Shamanism For "White" People
Reclaiming Our Animist Heritage

By
Michael William Denney

Introduction

At the time of this writing, I am in the process of writing a book entitled, "Mounting Sleipnir" which is a work focused on examining and resurrecting a modern form of pre-Christian Teutonic animism. As a writer and a teacher, I have a tendency to go off on tangents. I have come to accept this about myself and so I no longer try to censor my thought process. My goal for Mounting Sleipnir is to stay focused primarily on Teutonic and Indo-European animism.

However, as I have been writing that book, I have found myself wanting to explore more general subjects concerning animism. As it turns out, I have some strong feelings concerning current trends regarding modern animist practices. Many of those feelings kept trying to make their way into the 'Sleipnir' book.

In an attempt to keep that book on topic, I began writing my thoughts and feelings down in the form of short essays. My expectation was that I would get a couple of thoughts out at a time and then be able to focus on the book. But, instead, once I started this process, the thoughts kept flowing out of me very passionately. Within a few pages, I realized that there was a small book that wanted to get written. This is how "Shamanism for 'White' People" was born.

Neo-shamanism and animism are more popular now in the Western world than ever before. It is my passionate belief that reintegrating animism (shamanism) into our modern society is imperative if we are going to return our world to a state of balance and pull the human race back from the precipice upon which we are teetering.

But, I also firmly believe that it is important that we understand where we "white" people have come from so that we can understand what animism really is. We cannot simply project our modern mindset onto our pre-Christian European animist beliefs. We must first understand from an experiential level what our ancestors believed. My experience is that in order for us modern Westerners to fully understand the animism of our ancestors, we need to have a transformation of consciousness.

My journey to my own ancestral European animism started with 20 years of training in various foreign animist traditions with unbroken connections into prehistory. After 20 years of training in various animist lineages including the Taoist, Hindu, Vedic and Yoruba (West African) traditions, I was able to better absorb and understand the animist mythology of my Norse ancestors. In fact, I would say that those 20 years of training were mandatory for me to understand where my pre-Christian animist ancestors were coming from.

While I am gratified to see more and more modern Westerners embracing animism as a way of life, I am also concerned that we are simply imposing modern, dualist, Western values onto this deep and complex philosophy.

In this book, I will share many of my thoughts and reflections on some current trends in modern Western animism or "neo-shamanism." I have a tendency to be blunt about my passionate feelings. I have and continue to find ways to be more cooperative and constructive when sharing my perceptions. However, there is a time for "tough love."

For those who can hear it, I am going to share some tough love on both sides of this subject. I will likely offend everyone at some point in this book. That is not my intention, but as a warrior, I find it is good to clear the air once in a while.

If you are able to read the whole book, there is most likely some things we see eye to eye on. My main goal is to get people talking and communicating about these subjects as opposed to us all isolating in our own respective cliques and pointing at the other folks around us with whom we might disagree.

Well, this introduction is getting long-winded and I have not expressed what I wanted, so let's just get started, shall we?

This book is written in a specific order, but as with my other works, you are free to jump around.

Enjoy...

A Modern, Western "Shaman"

I practice a form of traditional, pre-Christian, European animism or what many people would describe as "shamanism." The word shamanism has been largely misunderstood in recent times. Modern neo-shamanism is actually more accurately defined as "animism." When the average person uses the word "shamanism," most of the time, whether they realize it or not, what they really mean is "animism" not shamanism.

What is Animism?

Animism is the belief that all of creation possesses a spirit and a consciousness. Animists believe that all things whether they be rocks, trees, animals, energies, ideas, etc., are all part of an interactive web of Life Force Consciousness Energy. Animists believe that all things seen and unseen can be interacted with and communicated with. The job of the animist practitioner is to act as an intermediary between the spiritual and physical realms. The animist understanding is that all of creation seeks a dynamic balance with itself. The animist strategy for survival is for humans to seek to a dynamic balance with the forces of creation surrounding them.

Animism was the first form of "religion" in the world and every culture on the planet can trace their spiritual origins to some form of animism. All religions being practiced today that still possess an unbroken connection into prehistory are animist in nature to some degree. I'll explore the definitions of

animism and shamanism later on, but, first, before I
do anything else...

Why "White" People?

My apologies for using the racially charged phrase
"white people" in the title. I am of northern
European descent or what some people would call
a "white" person. But, let me be clear. I'm not a
racist. I do not have any racial agenda. I couldn't
care less about anybody's skin color. I find the
racially charged term "white people" as divisive and
offensive as any other racial generalization. But, I
chose that term deliberately to get your attention
and hopefully start some meaningful dialogue about
what I believe is a very important subject. I'm not
going to pull any punches. I'm not going to talk
around the issues or allow racial stereotypes or
political correctness to distract me from talking
about what I consider to be the real issues behind
this subject that is very often overlooked among all
the heated rhetoric.

Animism is Our Birthright

Like many of you, I believe it is the fundamental
spiritual birthright for everyone regardless of culture
or ethnicity to practice authentic, earth-centered,
spiritual wisdom, if that is their choice. It is an
undeniable fact, however, that Western society has
abandoned and forgotten its traditional, Earth-
centered, animist spiritual heritage. In fact,
Europeans and their descendants have done such
a thorough job in recent centuries of discarding and

forgetting their own extremely ancient, ancestral, spiritual roots that many people in the Western world do not even know their ancestors practiced animism or "shamanism."

The modern monotheist religions of the Western world are not the traditional religions of northern Europe as is commonly believed. Monotheism is actually a very, very recent religious philosophy in human history and is in direct opposition to what has been the default religious and philosophical mindset of all humans throughout time, including Europeans.

Animist religions are largely perceived by Westerners as only being practiced by primitive, third-world cultures. But, in actuality, it has only been in the last one thousand years or so that our European ancestors abandoned their ancestral animist practices altogether. That means for at least 50,000 years, the ancestral spiritual tradition of all Europeans was very similar to all other animist religions in existence today including the religions of Native Americans, Siberians, Africans and East Indians - just to name a few.

Is Animism a "Foreign" Practice?
The fact that we Westerners no longer have a cultural memory of these animist traditions in our history has forced many who want to practice an authentic form of animism to look outside of their own culture for these types of traditions. Many

people have been very successful at finding and practicing authentic ancient traditions from different parts of the world. Many Westerners have been legitimately accepted into these spiritual traditions and have even been authorized to teach them to others. This has been very healing to many Westerners who have been able to reintegrate traditional animist understandings into their life and psyches.

The problem is that most Westerners do not even realize that they are heirs to some of the oldest animist traditions on the planet. The knee-jerk reaction for many is to assume that so called "white people" are somehow spiritually inferior when it comes to earth centered wisdom.

Truth be told, however, this reputation of the "soul-less white man" isn't entirely unjustified. But, it has nothing to with ethnicity. It is a cultural phenomenon. It is the result of a relatively recent dynamic born out of political, religious and military conflict that occurred during the Roman conquest of Europe and into the medieval era that lasted over the span of 1,000 years. This conflict, the true nature of which has been largely ignored by historians, resulted in the complete destruction of traditional European spirituality. This eradication of our ancestral philosophy has been catastrophic to the European psyche. The wounds of which we still carry like a plague and spread into every culture that we have connected with since that time.

The "Soul-less" White Man
It is a fact that many Westerners over the past five hundred years, as a result of the abandonment of their ancestral traditions, have engaged in some extremely destructive behavior towards our planet and our fellow humans. Abandoning our ancestors' beliefs have also resulted in thought patterns and mindsets that continue to plague much of Western society. Many Westerners are still continuing to blindly engage in extremely destructive practices to our ecosystem and our civilization. These practices, however, are often seen as integral to our modern survival. This misperception is a result of 1,000 years of aggressively distancing ourselves from our traditional animist beliefs.

Animism is an Evolutionary Human Adaptation
Animism is a mindset that has been hardwired into the human brain as a result of 100,000 years of human evolution. The animist world view was the default survival mechanism for all humans for tens of thousands of years. It is the instinctual survival strategy with which humans naturally interface with their environment.

Any human being, regardless of ethnic background will naturally adopt an animist mindset unless they are raised in a society that aggressively seeks to eradicate this belief system out of them. Modern Western society, religion and education systems go to great lengths to eradicate this instinctual animist survival strategy out of its citizens. The current Western mindset which opposes itself to the animist mindset is not born into us, it has to be learned over many years.

Children are often praised for their "imaginations." However, once they reach a certain age, they are aggressively taught to discard their natural animist instincts for what we refer to as the logical, scientific mind, or in many cases, the "righteous" monotheist religious mindset which is violently antagonistic to animism.

The instinctual animist mindset is one which perceives itself to be integrally interconnected to all of Creation. This is in direct opposition to the modern mindset in Western society which teaches that humans are separated from manifested reality.

The Invention of Spiritual Separation
This mindset of separation is derived from the institutionalized Christian religious teaching that "Man is separated from God." Human nature is perceived by Christianity to be "earthly." This creates an extreme dualist philosophy which pits humans in their natural state against the monotheist God. This understanding is reflected in the Christian belief that "Man is born in sin" and worthy of destruction from birth. It is Man's earth-bound "flesh" itself which is seen as the source of this sinfulness. Only through the sacrifice of God's son,

Jesus is any human considered by Christianity to be worthy of communion with God.

Yet, even after a person's conversion to this belief system, he/she is still considered fundamentally sinful but "forgiven." This double message of "sinful, but forgiven" creates in the human psyche a perpetual state of spiritual confusion and guilt. Any connection therefore between humans and the natural world on any level is considered sinful and aggressively demonized.

There is a phrase in Christianity known as the "natural man." This refers to the natural instincts inherent in all human beings. This "natural man" is treated by Christianity as a separate, sinful personality which the righteous Christian is encouraged to fight against and subdue.

Since the "natural man" is exactly what it describes, this creates a deep, self-hatred within the individual. Any natural instinct is labeled as "sinful" and is aggressively targeted by the individual for extermination. So, the individual who, by nature of their humanity, must feel natural impulses and drives every moment of his/her existence, also feels deep guilt for every honest feeling and impulse that he/she experiences. Any sense of "righteousness" is therefore, by definition, something that is artificially created and externally imposed onto the mind by the intellect.

The result is that the Christian mindset is one that is dominated by artificial, arbitrary, intellectual "righteous" values that the individual is constantly seeking to impose upon the "natural man" within.

This perception of perpetual "sinfulness" results in a deep psychological guilt, fear and antagonism toward anything "earthly" or connected to human physiological instincts. Since humans naturally have very powerful physical instincts, this creates an intense internal conflict.

Origins of Earth Antagonism in Western Society
Those who have been indoctrinated into this dualist, anti-earth mindset, in order to perceive themselves as spiritual, will aggressively attack anything in their external environment that has the potential to strengthen their connection to their natural selves or the natural world around them. Thus, we see the modern term "tree hugger" seemingly to describe an aberrant viewpoint, whereas the pre-Christian European tradition was instead, to sanctify Nature and seek transcendental spiritual fulfillment through Her.

Let us take the modern Christianized viewpoint that derides the so-called "tree-huggers" and compare it with the default, pre-Christian animist European mindset.

According to the Roman historian Tacitus, 2,000 years ago, the indigenous, animist Germanic tribes in Northern Europe were fundamentally different from what is considered to be the average mindset of "white people" today.

"...The Germanic tribes, however, do not consider it consistent with the grandeur of celestial beings to confine the gods within walls, or to liken them to the form of any human countenance. They consecrate woods and groves, and they apply the names of deities to the abstraction which they see only in spiritual worship."

This clearly shows that the traditional viewpoint of tribal Europeans was to observe divinity from within Nature Herself. The ancestral cultural tradition of indigenous Europeans was to preserve Nature rather than aggressively develop or destroy Her. The modern Western viewpoint which demonizes Nature, sees Her as an enemy to human survival which must be controlled and subdued is alien to the traditional European mindset. The widely accepted characterization of environmentalists as being abnormal must have been aggressively imposed upon the modern Western mind.
This anti-environmental dualism which fosters an antagonism to anything natural or "earthly" has been so deeply ingrained into the Western psyche that the entire modern Western culture has been founded upon it.

Traditional animism believes that the forces of both negative and positive are inextricably interconnected. Animists believe that a state of harmony is one where these opposing forces are balanced and harmonized rather than exterminated. The modern dualist mindset, however, assumes that Nature and all things natural are at war with humanity and must be conquered, controlled, exploited or even destroyed.

In order for early Christians to overcome indigenous animist belief systems in medieval Europe, missionaries adopted a very aggressive policy of demonizing any indigenous European practices or beliefs that reflected the traditional animist mindset. Traditional, sacred, sites were often renamed with the word "devil" by Christians to dissuade further animist worship. Such examples might include names like "devil's hill" etc., Christians would also take advantage of sacred pagan sites by building churches on top of them.

This practice of destroying indigenous sacred sites was not limited to Christians. This strategy was also employed by pre-Christian Roman conquerors. Invading Roman armies would routinely chop down sacred forests in tribal areas they sought to conquer in order to humiliate the local gods.

Many indigenous Europeans had powerful, ancient, cultural and spiritual ties to the land upon which they lived. By destroying their sacred forests, the Romans were seeking to humiliate and disempower the local deities and ancestors who were believed by the locals to be sources of great power. By killing the local ancestor spirits and nature deities, this would have the effect of severely diminishing any sense of spiritual power in the tribes who might seek the assistance of their local gods or ancestors in mounting any martial defense against the Roman invaders.

Without their ancestral deities to empower and protect them, such tribes were left without a spiritual heritage and were more likely to willingly integrate into Roman imperial culture. This practice by the Romans helped set the stage for introducing the imperial mindset of Europe that was significantly increased by the introduction of the belief in the monotheist, Christian god. Monotheism was an even more effective tool of imperialist Rome to unify disparate cultures into one vast empire.

As a result of hundreds of years of aggressive, institutionalized, Christian missionary campaigns to wipe out the indigenous, animist, European mindset, Western society now, unconsciously and, as a matter of course, indoctrinates its citizens from birth into the separatist mindset installed by empirical, institutionalized Christianity.

This mindset of separation pervades all of modern Western society and is not isolated to practicing monotheists any longer. Just because someone chooses to reject formalized monotheist religion, does not in and of itself, remove the deeply ingrained separatist thought patterns implanted into our subconscious minds. Even atheists, agnostics and alternative religions very often still operate unconsciously from the Western mindset that has been implanted into them. This mindset of separation has become fundamental to all of modern Western culture, education, religion, economics, medicine, etc... In point of fact, our entire modern civilization is fueled by the philosophy of separation.

The Emergence of Neo-Animism
But, since the natural, evolutionary instinct of all people is to operate from animism, and since this instinct is unbelievably powerful, more and more people will continue to seek out animism wherever they can find it.

This brings us to our current controversies surrounding "white people" and neo-shamanism. The current situation is this: There is a great deal of controversy over the increasing trend of people of European descent practicing various forms of neo-animism or "shamanism." Much controversy surrounds people who are referred to as "plastic shamans." These are people who openly profess to practice what they call "Native American Shamanism." Such people are viewed with derision by both Native Americans and conservative Westerners alike. As such, they feel like extreme outcasts and rebels who do not fit into any group.

Most likely these "plastic" shamans are of European descent and have been raised in an environment that was antagonistic to animist beliefs. Very often, they may have been indoctrinated into the belief that animism was unnatural to them. In addition, it is also very likely that they experienced their upbringing as being very oppressive and spiritually injurious to them. As a result, the desire to seek out animism is intensified by a perceived need on their part for mental and spiritual healing, even survival. Hence, their efforts have a desperation to them. Such people are not easily swayed from their goal to reintegrate animism into their lives. They feel that their very existence hinges upon finding and practicing what they believe to be "shamanism."

The so-called "shamanic" practice of "soul retrieval" is exceedingly pertinent in this scenario. These individuals have a very palpable sense that their natural animist souls have been forcibly removed by a society that they perceive as being antithetical to their very natures. These individuals have been convinced by modern Western society that such animist practices to reintegrate them on a psychological level do not exist in their own culture. Therefore, they automatically seek out practices in other cultures that are believed to remedy this serious problem.

Even though they are not of Native American descent, these individuals deeply identify with the victimization of Native Americans by "white," monotheist, Western culture. The Native American therefore becomes a symbol upon which these individuals can project their own feelings of victimization by that same culture. The stereotype of the Native American animist practitioner also provides these individuals with an identity that allows them to psychologically, culturally and spiritually separate themselves from the society that they feel has oppressed and harmed them.

If they believe, (as they have been taught to do) that the only way to experience the spiritual fulfillment that comes from earth wisdom is to search for it in other cultures, no amount of criticism will stop them in their quest. Any such criticism regardless of the source, will be viewed as another attempt to suppress them in their quest for spiritual and psychological fulfillment.

The instinctual drive to experience the feelings of connectedness with Nature and the Universe can no longer be suppressed in these individuals. They actively seek out the only forms of authentic animism that they believe they can find. Since the Native American culture has suffered so extensively at the hands of this same Western culture, these people feel an irresistible attraction to and sympathy with Native American spirituality.

This is one reason why there are so many false, Native American "shamans" who attract scores of followers. It is also why these individuals persist in appropriating Native American practices even though they have been sharply criticized by the Native American organizations whom, ironically, they are trying to emulate. In some cases, they have been threatened with law suits. But, even after acknowledging that their practices are not authentic, they still persist.

If these people are spiritually damaged as many of their detractors proclaim, then, the answer is not to attack or criticize them, but to give them access to what they seek. If Native Americans are understandably unwilling to allow outsiders access to their knowledge, then the solution to the problem is to provide authentic, alternative, animist spiritual practices to whomever needs them.

One way to solve this dilemma is to help people understand that they do not need to appropriate the cultural traditions of others to experience the benefits of authentic animism. It may be helpful for them to understand that whoever they are, and whatever their background is, they can seek out their own ancestors for Earth Wisdom. Even if their immediate ancestors did not follow animist practices, if one goes back far enough into anyone's ancestry, you will uncover someone who practiced an ancient and authentic form of animism or "shamanism."

The main goal of my work is to help people find authentic animist practices regardless of their ancestry. But, especially for those who are of European descent or who identify with Western or European culture, there is good news! There are a large number of sources readily available to help you to practice your own form of authentic "shamanic" Earth wisdom. (A brief list of resources will be provided at the end of this book.)

The First Humans In Europe Were Animists
The European people have been practicing animism for over 50,000 years. If you are of European descent, then animism is in your blood, in your veins, in your DNA. The unconscious assumption that Native American culture is superior to that of our European animist ancestors is destructive to our own spiritual identity and some would say is offensive to our ancestors and their traditional "shamanic" culture. This is one reason why many Native Americans are so offended and simultaneously mystified by this practice of spiritual appropriation. To indigenous animist cultures, it doesn't make sense to avoid one's own ancestors.

As a native Westerner, I understand why many of my brethren seek out foreign animism. It is because we have been robbed of our own animist history.

But what is most important for the reader to know is that appropriating the spiritual identity of another culture without permission is destructive to one's own spirit. If done with permission, learning foreign spiritual practices can be very healing. But, if done without permission, the individual not only brings offense to the Native American culture he/she seeks to emulate, but it also damages one's own spirit and brings sadness to one's own ancient ancestors who very much desire to share their power and wisdom with us.

Imagine if you wanted to share some wisdom with your grandson or granddaughter and they ignored you completely as though you never existed and went to your unrelated neighbor for love and attention. That is what is felt by our own ancestors when we simply ignore their existence and their hard-won wisdom. For 50,000 years, our ancestors worshipped Nature and those same animist masters are still available to us to help and guide us in this lifetime with their Earth wisdom.

Now, I personally, have no problem whatsoever with anyone practicing any form of spirituality of their choice; whether that be Native American or otherwise. I myself have studied in traditional practices from Africa, India and China and I have been accepted into those traditions by both the native practitioners and their respective deities and ancestors. (Yes, I had permission in all cases.) I also practice my own ancestral, pre-Christian European traditions. So, I am not proposing any kind of culturally exclusive spiritual practice.

Hey, if you can find a Native American Elder who wants to teach you and authorize you to teach.

More power to you. But the fact of the matter is that most Native Americans do not share their ancestral wisdom even with people from other Native American cultures. They simply do not want any outsiders practicing their traditions. Period!

Unlike the other cultural practices that I mentioned earlier that are very open about sharing their spirituality with foreigners, Native Americans have a very recent and painful history with Europeans and their descendants. By appropriating their traditions, it re-inflames very recent painful cultural memories. While we may not be aware of how simply seeking out a practice that we may desperately need and want can hurt them, it nevertheless is still destructive and contrary to the precepts held by all animists who seek healing and harmony with all beings.

The Solution Is Within YOU
Since spiritual appropriation is so destructive, why not, instead, find an Earth-centered practice that is readily available to you. All practicing animists will tell you that you have direct access to your own ancestors at any time. Seek them out and let them guide you.

Siberian Tengerism vs Neo-Shamanism
So, before I get any further into pre-Christian, European spiritual heritage, let us first examine some of the inaccurate information regarding the word "shamanism." It is important to be educated

about this word because it has been inaccurately used for centuries.

First, we need to understand that, in actuality, there is no such word as "shaman-ism." A shaman is an animist priest exclusive to the indigenous Siberian religion which is called "Tengerism." The appropriate term for authentic Siberian animism is "Tengerism" not "shamanism."

Secondly, according to Tengerism, no one can arbitrarily choose to become a shaman. The individual must be chosen by the ancestor spirits and then he/she must train with a recognized master shaman. This means that even native Siberians cannot call themselves a shaman until having been initiated and recognized as such by a master.

The reason the word "shaman" has come to refer to an animist priest in modern Western society is because this word was appropriated in the 17th century by Europeans who visited Siberia.

These European Christians witnessed indigenous Tengerist priests practicing their religion. Since by that point in time, Europeans had no cultural memory of the similar animist practices of their own ancestors just a few centuries earlier, they perceived the animist practices of the Tengerist priests as being exotic, primitive, superstitious and even "evil."

From this time on, European anthropologists began describing ANY indigenous animist practice as "shaman-ism." So, from the very beginning of the anthropological use of the term "shamanism," it was associated with a generalized definition of every animist practice regardless of cultural origin.

This is another reason why this term is so offensive to both Native Americans and Siberian Tengerists if used inaccurately. By arbitrarily calling something "shamanism" or "shamanic," it dilutes both the Siberian religion and whatever practice it attempts to describe.

"Animism" is an appropriate term for all the above practices because it is intended to be a generalized description. So, I propose that when anyone wishes to use the term "shamanism" to describe an animist practice, that we instead replace it with the terms "animist," "animism" or "animistic." By definition, Tengerism and many Native American practices can be accurately described as forms of animism.

This way, Native Americans, Tengerists and Westerners can find common ground to build upon and dialogue surrounding common animist understandings. We can acknowledge the shared similarities held by all animist practices without diluting or demeaning any of them.

While I do not speak for any Native Americans, I have made some observations: What seems to me to be one of the main issues with Native Americans is not that Westerners are seeking to practice animism, but that they are appropriating the cultural symbols, language and identities of Native American tribes without permission in an attempt to practice animism. It is my sense that most Native Americans would be happy to share general animist spiritual knowledge with fellow animists who are seeking to resurrect their OWN ancestral animist practices. Such shared knowledge might be incorporated into these resurrected European animist practices as long as we used our own symbolism.

Any Native American Wisdom Keepers who wish to confirm or deny this impression I have is encouraged to contact me. In fact, if this book finds its way to any authentic Native American spiritual practitioners and you would like to work together with me in helping to educate people in this regard, you are invited to contact me.

In my opinion, the perceived need of Westerners to appropriate foreign animism stems from a deep spiritual insecurity by Westerners whose ancestors themselves were victims of cultural and spiritual genocide at the hands of Roman imperialists and later, Christian missionaries.

The Roman and Christian Oppression of Indigenous European Animists

Many people may not realize it, but the same kind of ethnic, spiritual and cultural genocide that has been visited upon Native American cultures and other indigenous cultures by Europeans over the past 500 years was also visited upon northern European animist tribes and cultures 2,000 years ago by Roman invaders and then later, Christian missionaries. Let me share three examples. Bear in mind that these three instances are just the tip of the iceberg in terms of the 2,000 years of oppression against animism in the Western world.

Destruction of The Druids

In 43 A.D., Rome invaded Celtic Britain. During the resulting occupation that lasted for 400 years, the Roman army completely wiped out the indigenous Druid population.

Even though the Romans were a superior military force, the Druid priests held powerful influence over the native Celtic tribes. Even though they were outgunned, the native Celts believed that the power of the Druid priests would be able to drive out the Roman invaders. The Druids used their influence to continue to stir up rebellions among the native Celts. So, to deal with this constant annoyance, the Roman army massacred all of the Druids. The Druids were literally driven over a cliff into the sea. Rome occupied Britain for 400 more years until the arrival of the Saxons.

The Gothic War

In 376 A.D., invading Huns, drove the Germanic Gothic tribes to the edge of Roman territory. The Romans had, up until that time, been using Gothic warriors as mercenaries against each other. Rome had made and broken several treaties with them. Thousands of Goths had been taken into slavery. This had been going on for hundreds of years between Rome and the tribal Goths. But, the Huns were now massacring them and had driven them from their homeland.

So, the desperate Goths had no choice but to seek asylum in the safety of the Roman empire. After being lawfully admitted into the Roman Empire and promised territory, food and military protection from the invading Huns, the Germanic Gothic tribes were placed by Rome in concentration camps and denied food while their men were used as human shields in the Roman army. Gothic children were sold into slavery in exchange for dog meat.

The Gothic tribes, then, desperately asked Rome for help and were told to endure a long march to the Roman city of Marcianople where they were promised to be given food and supplies. After a long march that killed many of the sick and starving Goths, the Marcianople Garrison refused them entry and then tried to assassinate Gothic leaders during a banquet in their honor. The Goths rebelled and defeated the Roman garrison at Marcianople.

The Goths, then went to other Roman towns seeking food and instead were greeted with Roman troops. In each instance, the hungry, desperate Goths defeated the Roman soldiers sent against them. Eventually, the Goths made their way to Rome itself still seeking food. The Goths had successfully defeated the entire Western Roman military presence and this left Rome defenseless. Rome still refused to give food the Goths, so they surrounded the city. Months later, someone opened the gates, the Goths entered the city to find that there was no food or supplies left. Enraged, they "sacked" the city. The Goths had never intended on sacking Rome. All they wanted was a place to live and the means to make a living. With no homeland, no food and no supplies, they had no choice but to rebel.

Rome never recovered. All because they broke their word.

This is the way our tribal ancestors were treated by the Roman empire for hundreds of years. As with many conquered and oppressed cultures, the Romanized Germanic tribes adopted the ways of their oppressors.

Massacre of Saxon Pagans
In 782, the Holy Roman Emperor, Charlemagne was responsible for the "Verden Massacre" where

4,500 indigenous pagan Saxon cheiftans were lured into a trap and executed.

Charlemagne was having difficulty conquering the last indigenous Germanic pagans and converting them to Christianity. The Saxon pagan tribes on the outskirts of Charlemagne's territory repeatedly rebelled against his authority simply because they were not willing to convert to Christianity. They were willing to ally themselves to Charlemagne. They just didn't want to abandon their ancestral faith. Charlemagne demanded that all his subjects become Christians. The Saxon tribes refused.

So, Charlemagne simply slaughtered them all. He invited 4,500 Saxon chieftans to a peace meeting. Ancestral Saxon tradition prohibited warriors from bringing weapons to peace meetings. In tribal Saxon tradition, it was unthinkable for anyone to commit acts of violence at peace meetings. Such an act would be considered the epitome of cowardice by a Saxon warrior. The Saxon warrior code demanded truth in deed and word. Charlemagne (himself a descendant of the Germanic Frankish tribes) knew this. So, when the chieftans and their attendants arrived to the peace meeting, Charlemagne's army (who were fully armed) surrounded them, forced them to convert to Christianity and then executed them all. Sound familiar? Is it any wonder where European Americans learned how to break peace treaties and impose their religion onto others?

These are just three brief examples in a long history where the Roman imperial mindset was responsible for the destruction of the animist way of life in Europe.

Roman Legacy in Europe
Beginning in 58 BC, the Roman Empire began a campaign of military conquest, cultural genocide, racism, slavery and oppression in Europe that officially lasted for over 450 years until Rome was sacked by Germanic "barbarian" tribes. But even though the Roman Empire began it's official demise in 410 A.D., the spiritual genocide continued at the hands of the institutionalized Christian church up until the present time.

Romans, even before the arrival of Christianity branded all non-Romans (especially animists) as being inferior, primitive and superstitious. (The word "pagan" is a Roman word that translates into modern English as "ignorant, uneducated, superstitious redneck"). As has happened in more recent history with cultures that have been absorbed by Modern European Christian countries, the indigenous European tribal cultures that were conquered or absorbed by Roman civilization were taught to despise their pre-Roman, "barbarian" animist culture and beliefs.

Even though classical Rome was not able to conquer any territory north of France and Britain, eventually all of Europe adopted the Roman cultural and religious way of life. Even after the "fall" of the Roman empire, animist Europeans were routinely slaughtered in the thousands by successive invading armies of the "Holy Roman" Christian emperors.

The last practitioners of indigenous European spirituality lived in western Lithuania. They were forcibly converted to Christianity in 1413. But, indigenous European animism died hard. The Christian church and the monarchs that were supported by it continued to aggressively seek the complete eradication of animism from the European psyche. The continued spiritual destruction of the indigenous European animist mindset is most well known by the brutality of the Catholic inquisition and, in more recent times, the European and colonial American witch trials of the 17th century.

So, what we see now that has happened to Native Americans in recent history also happened to indigenous European animists. We have simply forgotten about it. Our ancestors ingested this disease of self-hatred and continued to spread it to others.

There is a saying in Twelve Step Recovery circles which says, "Hurt people - hurt people." This means that those who have been abused will often abuse others in similar fashion. This does not excuse anyone, but it does explain it. Since Western society is still infected to a large degree with this spiritual disease of spiritual and ancestral self-hatred, the only lasting answer is to admit and address this issue.

Since both European Americans and Native Americans are connected to each other in the effects of this spiritual disease, I believe that it is beneficial for both sides to examine all aspects of our shared history. While we can choose to isolate and lick our own wounds, it is my hope that we can all engage in dialogue about these issues together and seek mutual healing as fellow animists.

Having said that, we each must be responsible for our own spiritual recovery. For Westerners, this means that we need to seek out our own cultural and spiritual healing first. On a spiritual level, this means that we Westerners must seek out our own ancestors for healing and, yes, even forgiveness. My experience in my personal ritual work leads me to believe that our tribal, European ancestors are deeply hurt by our abandonment of them and their wisdom. I have also experienced that they are very eager to teach us their knowledge. But, we must ask them for it. They will not impose it upon us.

Many of our animist ancestors suffered through intense hardship as they were forced through violence to renounce their animist beliefs. So, there is still much healing that needs to take place in the ancestral realm. It is my sense that some of our ancestors are confused and even lost. By reawakening our ancestral practices, they can find their way in the spirit realm. It is my belief that much of our current difficulties, (economic, social and environmental) can be alleviated by sending healing to our ancestors on the spiritual plane.

Perpetuating Spiritual Confusion
By seeking to escape into Native American cultures without having addressed our own ancestral guides, we perpetuate the separation of ourselves from our ancestors. This does not mean that we cannot practice spirituality from other cultures, it simply means that if we are not able to accept ourselves for who we are, regardless of ethnic origins, we will never be truly whole on a spiritual level.

In such cases, if we do not address our own ethnic spiritual tragedies, it will not matter which spirituality we adopt, there will still be an emptiness that will bring a superficiality to whatever we practice. This is another aspect to why Native Americans take such deep offense at "plastic shamanism." Because they are able to profoundly sense the superficiality in the appropriated versions of plastic shamanism.

If those of us of European descent can accept that we are naturally and instinctually animist, just like everyone else, then we will no longer feel the need to adopt the culture of others in an attempt to absorb their animist beliefs. I believe, if we can accomplish this, we can heal the misunderstandings of our Native American cousins and gain what we initially wanted which is to find common ground between us all within animism in general.

The "Noble Savage"
I believe much of the allure of so-called "Native American Shamanism" is the stereotype of the primitive, skin-clad, "noble savage." Who doesn't like this idea? In all seriousness, I am not criticizing this. I am very attracted to the concept of the freedom associated with this stereotype. But, why do we assume that this is not part of our heritage? Why, when we want to embody this principle do we automatically assume that in order to access this, we must dress in Native American regalia?

In modern society, when we think of the stereotype of the civilized person who is disconnected with nature, what comes to mind? Someone of European descent, right? More often, this stereotype is associated with the American of Anglo-Saxon descent. The irony here is that the pre-Roman Germanic tribes (from whom many Americans are descended) were stereotyped by "civilized" Romans as the extreme example of the noble savage during the Roman empire.

When first encountered by the Romans, the Germanic tribes did not use money. They had no concept of money. They only bartered real goods with each other. Wealth was only reflected in cattle. Our English word "fee" comes from the Germanic word for cattle. Even nowadays when we receive payment for a service (a fee), we still used this same word for cow.

Caesar and Tacitus report that Germanic tribes wore mainly animal skins and bathed every morning in streams and rivers. They rode their horses bareback. They preferred to hunt and fish as opposed to farming. They had no cities. They lived in natural settings. They were utterly free of routine and simply did whatever they wanted. They were deeply spiritual people who received spiritual messages from horses. They listened to the call of birds for omens. They heavily practiced divination. Almost anything that we associate with the stereotypical Native American 'Medicine Man' was how the Romans perceived the Germanic tribes.

Germanic people were extremely friendly to travelers and visitors. Anyone seeking food or shelter was warmly welcomed and fed. It was considered extremely rude to refuse a request from anyone. They were proud that in their territories, the Germanic tribes had hundreds of miles of pristine wilderness on their borders.

They were fierce warriors who lived by a code of honor. They believed that their spirit was connected to their words. The worst thing an indigenous Germanic warrior could possibly do was to lie. To do so would negate their own existence. A Germanic tribal warrior would die before he broke his oath.

When traveling through sacred woods, one was expected to be completely silent. If someone fell down while traveling through a sacred grove or forest, they were required to crawl the rest of the way in order not to disturb the Nature spirits.

When visiting dignitaries from "civilized" countries would offer them gifts of money, the German tribes preferred silver to gold, because silver was shinier. They had no concept of the worth of coin money. When given silver goblets, it is recorded that the Germanic tribes preferred to drink from their wooden goblets instead.

They were reported to be innocent and without guile. Tacitus and Caesar both report that the Germanic tribes did not own anything including land. They had no slaves. They had no kings. Chiefs were not despots. All decisions were made through community voting. Roman women, in order to look more attractive to Roman men, would bleach their hair blonde in order to look like the "sexy, exotic, German slave girl."

I could go on but you get the point. If we read Tacitus's Germania and substitute "German" with "Native American" or whatever ethnicity reminds you of the stereotypical noble savage, the results are identical. So, if what we want is to reconnect to the tribal shaman, all we need to do is look to our own ancestors and emulate them.

The "Reader's Digest" Version of Animism

For those people not familiar with the "reader's digest" publication, it is a publication that among other things was known for its condensed version of popular novels. It was a way for a person to glean the basic storyline of novels without having to read the entire book with all its complexity and nuances. They were very similar to cliff's notes. Neo-shamanism tends to remind me of those condensed novels.

Neo-shamanism is almost entirely focused on two limited aspects of animism:
Trance vision experiences
Animist healing practices

I'm not seeking to denigrate these two practices. They are very important. My point is that traditional animism has much, much more to it. Neo-shamanism has boiled down the animist experience to only a small percentage of what is traditionally contained in complete traditions that can trace their connections into prehistory.

We modern Westerners make such a big deal about trance induced experiences and animist healing and label these practices as being exclusive to "shamanism." But every traditional spiritual practice teaches these two skills (including Christianity). To focus on these two skill-sets as the entirety of shamanism is like saying that auto mechanics only change the oil. Sure, the oil change happens very often, but there is much, much more to maintaining a car than just changing the oil. True animism in every culture has always been a deep and multifaceted practice where trance states and healing are but a small portion.

Redefining "Shamanism"
While it is my desire to see the popular use of the word "shamanism" changed to "animism," it is a regrettable fact that most Westerners unwittingly still use the word 'shamanism' outside of its original context. The term animism is less well known and is not as "cool." So, it may be a long while before the misuse of the word shamanism has stopped. Until such time, those of us who know better can gently educate anyone we come across who uses the word incorrectly.

I will continue to use this word "shamanism" publicly to gain attention to this issue simply because so few people are familiar with the term "animism." I am letting the reader know in advance that it may seem that I am using this phrase opportunistically to gain attention. I am doing so deliberately because those whom I feel that need to either be educated or participate in this discussion will most likely not be attracted to the accurate term of animism.

Moreover, most people get their information from internet search engines. And if someone is unaware of the meaning of animism, they simply will type in "shamanism" into search engines instead and never find this information. So, I am consciously and deliberately using the term "shamanism" so that this body of work concerning animism will pop up on their radars. So, please forgive me if I contradict my own advice and continue to use the term "shamanism" in future teachings, websites and products. I promise that I will always use the opportunity to reeducate people into the correct understanding of animism and away from pseudo-shamanism.

So, now let us examine the ancient origins of all Europeans.

Indo-European Animism
If you are descended from anyone who hails from any part of Europe, Northern India, Anatolia (Turkey), Iran and parts of Central Asia or even parts of the Middle East, you most likely are ethnically of "Indo-European" descent.

The Indo-European (IE) language is extremely old. Until recently we thought that the IE language was at least 7-10 thousand years old. But, in recent decades, science has concluded that the IE language is at least 50,000 years old. The first IE speakers migrated into the northern hemisphere from East Africa and spread into all of the geographical areas previously mentioned.

So, the fact of the matter is that if you are of IE descent, you can trace your language and pre-Christian animist religion all the way back to the first modern humans who migrated out of Africa. For more information on the genesis of the IE people, google the phrase "Paleolithic Continuity Paradigm."

So, as far as being an ancient animist culture, the IE culture is as old and authentic as it gets. Now, of course, the ethnicity of the IE people has changed considerably over tens of thousands of years due to adaptation to varying climactic conditions. But, our language and animist religious concepts have remained remarkably intact. Our first IE ancestors had dark skin, but after interbreeding with Neanderthals, (who carried the gene for light eyes, light skin and red hair) and after migrating into harsh Ice Age conditions that lasted for 40,000 years, the original IE skin pigment lightened considerably in some of the IE tribal communities in Europe. This is why the northern European branch of IE people have their distinctive light skin pigmentation.

But even though our physical appearance adapted to the climactic conditions in ice age Europe, our IE language has stayed relatively intact since our first ancestors left the African motherland.

Did you know that the oldest art in the world is found in Europe? Caves in modern day France and Germany contain stone age cave paintings that are at least 25,000 - 30,000 thousand years old. The oldest carved figurines in the world are found in this same region and date to the same period.

The oldest musical instruments in the world are finely carved flutes made from mammoth bone and bird wing-bones from these same caves dating back to the same time period. The people who created these artifacts are the ancestors of modern Europeans. They spoke IE. This is your spiritual heritage. You do not need to identify with anyone else to tap into very ancient, primal, animist spirituality. Our ancestors are still with us and they can be honored and sought after for spiritual guidance.

Indo-European Animist Core Beliefs and Concepts
So now, let's take a look at the general beliefs of the pre-Christian Indo-European people. These fundamental core beliefs were held by all IE tribes stretching from India to Scandinavia.

Many of the concepts infused into new age neo-shamanism which are often falsely attributed to Native American "shamanism" are already contained within prehistoric IE animism. Once again, it is unnecessary to seek for these concepts outside of our own heritage.

Let us take a look at some common spiritual concepts presumed by neo-shamanism to only be found in so-called "shamanic" cultures:

Father Sky
Mother Earth
World Tree
Thunder Being
Ancestor Spirits
Totem Spirits
Shapeshifting
Shamanic Journeying
Medicine Wheels
Vision Quest

These concepts are fundamental to traditional IE animism. Since my ancestry is mostly Scandinavian, Anglo-Saxon and Germanic, I will focus most of my examples in this area. However, the reader is encouraged to research any other pre-Christian traditions that attracts them.

Sky Father
The IE tribes believed in a Sky Father who lived in the North Star. By the light of the North Star, he guided all of humanity in their physical and spiritual destinies. In modern English, his name would be best rendered as "Day Father." The roots of these two words are seen in other IE names for this same

deity: Dyaeus Pita, Jupiter, Zeus, Tyr, Tiw and Ziu, just to name a few. The Roman god Ju-piter is a contraction of Dyeu (Sky) + Piter (Father).

Modern English	Sanskrit (India)	Roman	Greek
Day Father	Dyaeus Pita	Ju-Piter (Dyeu-Piter)	Zeus (Dzyeus)

Anglo-Saxon	German	Norse
Tiw	Ziu	Tyr

The Germanic names for Sky Father show an even older IE version where the Sky Father is simply referred to as "Tiw" which is cognate with the words "Day" and "Divinity" (Div-inity). The Sky Father was the source of pure celestial power as expressed in the stars, hence his Germanic name "Tiw" which could be translated as "Star," "Deity," "Sky," "Shining" or "Divine."

Earth Mother
The feminine counterpart to the masculine Sky Father was the Earth Mother. There are different names for the Earth Mother in different IE languages but the fundamental concept still applied. The Earth Mother is the consort of the Sky Father. She gives birth to all the creatures and most of the gods. In some traditions, the Earth Mother even gives birth to the Sky Father.

The Earth Mother is often seen as a primordial force even more powerful than the gods. She is the source of all magic, creation and mystery. The oldest religious figurines in the world are Earth Mother figures found in caves in Northern Europe. These "fertility" idols are 25,000 years old. This indicates that Mother Earth my have been the first deity to be worshipped by modern humans. It was your Paleolithic IE ancestors who very possibly discovered the concept of the Earth Mother.

Examples of Earth Mother in prehistoric IE cultures:

Sanskrit	Germanic	Norse	Anglo-Saxon
Prithvi	Hulda, Hertha	Urd	Earth

Prithvi was the consort of "Dyeus Pita" the Vedic Sky Father. She was the mother of both Agni the Sacred Spiritual Fire and Indra, the Thunder God.

Mother Hulda or Mother Holle is the Earth Mother of the pre-historic continental Germanic tribes. Frau Holle is still celebrated in Germany today. Her name means "Hidden." Even to this day, German children are told the story of how Mother Holle brought an oppressed step child into her underground magical world through a sacred well and taught her the value of respect for life and hard work. The little girl respected the value of Mother Holle's world. As a result, the little girl was sent back up to the middle world with an abundance of gold. The wicked stepmother seeing the gold given to the step child, sends her own lazy daughter down the well. But the selfish daughter shows no respect for anything in the underworld and is sent back to the middle world empty-handed and covered in tar.

In Anglo-Saxon and Scandinavian traditions, one name for the Earth Mother is simply "Urd" or "Earth." We still use this word today to describe the life-giving soil beneath our feet as well as the planet on which we live.

But, the goddess Earth was much more than just a fertility goddess. She was the primordial Giantess from which all things emerged, including all of the gods and goddesses. She was the law of the Origin of all things.

The three most powerful forces in the Anglo-Saxon and Norse religion were Earth (Origin), Verdandi (Coming into Being) and Should (Future.) These three mighty Giantesses were the three fold law of karmic action and reaction. Every thing we think and do now in this moment becomes an energetic pattern in the Past (Earth) which influences the present moment (Verdandi) and results in future consequences (Should.) This triune force of past, present and future was called Weird (Wyrd).

The Giantesses of Wyrd, wove the entire Cosmos into being. Nowadays, "weird" means something strange or supernatural. But to our ancestors, Wyrd meant the Life-force Energy Web that encompasses all things including Time and Space. We still use this word "weird" every single day. The European concept of the interconnectedness of all Life-force Energy is so integral to our thought patterns that even Christianity could not erase it from our daily vocabulary.

World Tree
A fundamental concept found in many animist religions is the "World Tree." Various "shamanic" religions (including some native, pre-Christian European traditions) contain the belief that there are multiple dimensions or "worlds" that are housed within a multi-branched tree. Neo-shamanism focuses on three worlds: the upper, middle and lower world. In actuality, however, there are usually nine worlds associated with the world tree.

The Siberian Tengerist religion from which the word "shaman" is derived, has nine branches in its world tree. This coincidentally corresponds with the pre-Christian Scandinavian world tree "Yggdrassil" which also has nine worlds. The "shamanic" three worlds in this tree are represented by the upper world called "Asgard" or "Fortress of the Celestial gods," the middle world called "Midgard" or "Middle Fortress" or as it is more commonly known - "Middle Earth," and the underworld called "Hel."

Christianity appropriated the pre-Christian Germanic underworld Hel and converted it into a place of eternal torment. However, in pre-Christian Germanic animism, Hel was the underworld where human souls went after death to prepare for rebirth in Middle Earth. Hel was predominantly a place of healing and regeneration. Some souls who had committed atrocities while in Middle Earth underwent temporary self-induced punishment. But there never existed a place of eternal torment in traditional pre-Christian European religions.

Thunder Being
All prehistoric IE cultures had a version of a Thunder god. Sometimes the Sky Father had a dual role of both Sky Father and Thunder God. The Roman god, Jupiter and the Greek god, Zeus were modeled after this dual Sky Father role.

Other IE traditions had a separate deity whose sole function was that of Thunder God. Examples of the latter type of Thunder god are seen in the Celtic "Taranis," The Vedic "Indra," the Anglo-Saxon "Thunor" and the Scandinavian "Thor." In these latter examples, the Thunder god is usually the son of the Sky Father and Earth Mother.

Ancestor Spirits
Honoring the ancestors is fundamental to all original spiritual traditions regardless of culture. The IE traditions are no exception to this rule. The

Germanic traditions are filled with different types of ancestor worship. I will list a few examples.

Hamingja Spirits
The Hamingja is a pre-Christian Scandinavian concept. The Hamingja was an ancestral spirit that was invited into the family home to protect and bring prosperity. The word "Hamingja" is often translated as "luck." A person's luck was thought to be inherited from one's ancestors. Humans were encouraged to welcome and honor the Hamingja as a family member.

People could choose to accept or reject a Hamingja spirit. One Viking account of a Hamingja spirit encounter even suggests that a Hamingja spirit could be adopted by another person if the intended recipient rejects his Hamingja.

Elves
The word "elf" can have different meanings. Some elves are mischievous or even harmful. However, the most revered of the elven beings were called the "Light-Elves."

According to my research, elves in general are powerful nature spirits But, the Light Elves fill the role of ascended spiritual masters who guide the human race toward spiritual evolution. Elves also had a strong ancestral connection. While the Hamingja spirits were more concerned with influencing one's physical prosperity, the Elves were more connected to influencing one's spiritual state of being. Tolkien's version of the Elf race in his "Lord of the Rings" books was modeled after the traditional pre-Christian understanding of the Light-Elves.

Elf Sacrifice

In pagan Scandinavia, autumn was dedicated to Elf worship. During the night of the Elf Sacrifice, Christians were not allowed into pagan households because to do so would bring down the curses of the Elves and Odin.

One medieval historical account records that some Christians traveling through pagan Scandinavia were caught in a storm and sought shelter in a pagan house. They did not know that this night was the "Alfablot" or "Elf Sacrifice." In each instance, the Christians were rudely and sometimes violently chased away by pagan householders. This is interesting because the pre-Christian pagan tradition was to never refuse refuge to a stranger. To refuse hospitality to a stranger was a very serious spiritual offense in pagan society. However, in each instance, the Christians were chased away.

The pagan understanding was that Christians had abandoned their ancestors and brought ancestral anger onto them. The pagans wanted to make sure that the Elves did not mistake them for Christians.

So, for pagans to chase off anyone shows how deeply they revered the Elves.

But, what about Santa's elves? Let me dispel some modern misunderstandings concerning these beings. Elves are not tiny sprites or those little people that build toys for Santa. These are representations of modern elves that are actually modeled after the pre-Christian Germanic entities knowns as dwarves. Elves and dwarves are completely different spirit beings.

Stone Circles and Ancestor Worship
Many people may not be aware of one of the main functions of Stone Circles in pre-Christian Europe. Besides being used for observing celestial events such as solstices and equinoxes, stone circles were also temples to the ancestors. Archeological excavations in Stonehenge have revealed that cremated remains were buried underneath the stones.

During the Viking era, community elders would gather in local stone circles for important meetings where community decisions were made. They gathered at these circles in order to have their consciousness influenced by the presence of the deceased ancestors who dwelt in those circles. It was well known by Vikings that the ashes of powerful deceased leaders were buried on those stone circle sites.

Totem Spirit

One of the most popular neo-shamanic practices is to discover one's "totem spirit." According to neo-shamanism, a person's totem will be an animal spirit used as a guide and protector in "shamanic journeys."

Here we have another misapplication of words. "Totem" is a word from the Ojibwe tribe which means "ancestral or family spirit." A totem could also be a personal power symbol. Once again, neo-shamanism has appropriated a term specific to one Native American culture and applied it arbitrarily to all Native American and "shamanic" cultures.

According to neo-shamanism, the totem is a personal spirit, often an animal, assigned to a person at birth that helps, protects and guides the individual throughout their life. Contacting and working with one's totem spirit is one of the main focuses of neo-shamanic practices.

Fetch Spirit

The concept of a personal helper spirit is also represented in pre-Christian European spirituality. In the Germanic traditions, the helper spirit was known as a "Fetch" (English) or "Fylja" (Norse.) A fetch spirit was often represented as an animal. The fetch would usually appear to the individual in dreams. If a fetch was seen while a person was awake, it was considered a bad omen and may portend a person's impending death. If a fetch was represented as a female human, then it was considered a guardian spirit of one's family or clan.

When I was seven years old, I almost died from scarlet fever. One night, I awoke to see a female spirit standing in my bedroom doorway. She was transparent and highly luminous. She sat on the edge of my bed and told me about my future. Shortly after her appearance, my fever broke and I began to recover from that moment on. When I asked about the experience, I was told by my parents that the woman was my guardian angel. My Anglo-Saxon ancestors would have identified her as a guardian fetch spirit connected to my clan.

Familiar Spirit
In medieval Europe, a familiar spirit was considered to be a spirit helper used by witches to accomplish their magical rites. A "familiar" was often represented as an animal but could also take the form of a human, humanoid or even a mythical creature.

Familiar spirits were often times gifted to an individual by a family member or fellow magical practitioner. These kinds of familiars would often appear when the individual was in physical danger to guide or protect them.

The obvious conclusion here is that it is completely unnecessary for modern Westerners to look outside of their own culture for the totem concept. I am of the belief that this concept of the spirit helper is so deeply ingrained in the European psyche that our modern neo-shamanic obsession with them is actually our own ancestral memories of this practice seeking a means of expression. Since most moderners have not been taught that spirit guides and protectors are part of the European spiritual heritage, we instinctively seek out foreign practices that can reunite us with our personal and clan protectors.

Shapeshifting
This is another concept that has often times been identified solely with "shamanism." Shapeshifting was widely practiced in Pre-Christian Europe.

Berserkers
Our modern phrase to "go berserk" comes from the Viking age practice of warriors who would summon the power of the bear or wolf in battle. A Berserker would put themselves into a state of deep trance where the power of the animal would possess their bodies and make them invincible in battle. The word "berserk" is a compound of two words; Ber (*bear) + serk (coat).* So, a Berserker is literally "someone who wears a bear coat." Berserkers would typically wear the pelt of either a wolf or a bear into battle. The Berserker clearly reflects a very ancient animist shapeshifting practice among the Germanic tribes.

There are other legends concerning the ability of some Viking warrior-wizards who had the ability to shapeshift in what we would describe as "shamanic journeying" with dramatic results in the 'real world.' According to the legends, these warrior-wizards would "go to sleep" in a location adjacent to the battlefield. At the precise time that the warrior or wizard was sleeping, bears or wolves magically appeared on the battlefield and participated in the fighting. Once the warrior awoke from his trance, the spirit animals mysteriously disappeared.

Witches reportedly had the ability to become birds or other animals and travel to distant locations for their magical works.

Instances of shape-shifting in European animism is very prevalent. All one needs to do is a small bit of research to discover the depth of this belief in Western culture.

Shamanic Journeying
A great example in the European tradition of what we might consider as a 'shamanic journey' is reflected in the pre-Christian Norse myth *"The Mocking of King Gylfe."*

"King Gylfe was a wise and knowledgeable man. He wondered how the Asa-people (star people) were so knowing that all went according to their wishes. He considered that this was caused either by the Asa-people's own nature or was brought about by the gods to whom they sacrificed. He determined to find this out and prepared to travel to Asgard (the upper world) in all secrecy, disguised as an old man. But the Asa-people were wiser. They saw his journey before he

came and caused him to be beset by illusions. When he arrived at the court he saw a hall so high that he could barely see the top of it. Its roof was covered with golden shields as other roofs might be with shingles.

At the entrance to the hall he saw a man seven small swords at once. Gylfe was asked his name and gave it as Ganglare (wandering learner), said he had come by watery ways (by sea) and wished to find lodging here. He then asked whose hall it was. The juggler replied it belonged to the king, "and I shall take you to see him," he said, "so that you yourself can ask his name."

The man walked into the hall; Gylfe followed. At once the door closed behind him. He saw many rooms and many people, some at games, some at drink, others with weapons at swordplay.

He saw three high seats, one above the other, with three figures seated, one on each. He asked what names these chieftains had and his conductor replied that he who sat in the lowest high seat was a king named "The High One"; the one above him was named "As High", and the uppermost was simply named "Third."

The High One asked the stranger his errand; and at his disposal were food and drink as for all in the High One's hall.

Gylfe said he first wanted to know if there was any wise man to be found. The High One replied that he would not leave the place whole were he not the wiser, and initiated the interrogation:

*'Step forward as you question.
Seated shall be the respondent.'*

Then, King Gylfe is told many wise sayings which are contained in a separate myth entitled, *"The Words of the High One."* At the end of that myth we are told how Gylfe returns to the world of Men...

"...King Gylfe, calling himself "Wandering Learner", heard all these things.

At length the High One spoke: "If you can ask still further, I know not whence you find the questions, for I never heard further forward the destinies of ages told. Enjoy therefore what you have learned."

Wandering Learner then heard a powerful thunderclap from all sides and looked out through the door; and as he looked about him he found himself on a level plain with no court or hall in sight.

So he returned to his country and told these tidings he had heard and seen. And after him, these sayings were passed on from one to another."

Woden (Odin) The "Shaman"

Woden is the Germanic god of ecstatic spiritual consciousness. His name means "Master of Wod" or "Master of Spiritual Fury." In modern English we still exclaim "Wow!" when we experience something awe inspiring. I am of the belief that this word 'wow' is derived from the same root as the ancient Germanic concept of 'Wod.'

Woden is renowned for his ability to travel to all of the nine worlds of the Tree of Life. The Germanic World Tree was named "Yggdrassil" which means "Ygg's Mount." Ygg is another name for Woden. The name "Ygg" also means "fury." Ygg comes from the same Indo-European root word as the Sanskrit word "Ugra." Coincidentally, Ugra is also one of the names of Shiva, the Hindu god of ecstatic spiritual consciousness.

Yggdrassil is the name for both the World Tree and Woden's horse. The obvious connection is that Woden is able to mount or ride the World Tree as one would mount a horse. Horses were also highly revered creatures in Germanic tribal society. Wizards were known to receive communications from the spirit world through horses. The Rune "Ehwaz" (Equus) is a very sacred Rune that is closely connected to communication with the spirit realm. The concept of the psychic union between horse and rider was symbolic of the human who has been 'mounted' by the gods.

Woden's horse Sleipnir (Slipper) has eight legs with which he "slips" in and out of all the nine worlds. Woden represents the earthly consciousness of humans. As such, Woden represents awareness in the world of men or what the Germanic tribes called "middle earth." So, Slipper's eight legs represent the other eight spiritual worlds of the World Tree. Woden is the evolved human consciousness in the middle realm that has the ability to travel ecstatically to the other non-human realms of the World Tree.

When Woden mounts Slipper we get the sacred number of nine (Woden + Slipper's eight legs = Nine worlds.) Yggdrassil is simultaneously the World Tree and Woden's horse because when Woden mounts the World Tree in ecstatic trance, he takes on another persona called "Ygg" or "The Furious One." Hence, the World Tree is named, "Ygg's Mount."

"Ugra" is often prefixed to Hindu deities as a way to describe them as "furious." This may sound frightening to us, but this description of furious really means that the deity in question, (i.e. Ugra-Tara etc), is the active form of the deity that is solely focused on spiritual purity.

Such a deity can be considered dangerous to humans because humans often have dual natures whereas the Ugra deities are so overwhelmed by their state of spiritual ecstacy, they are singly focused on spiritual evolution.

These gods are so "furiously" focused on spiritual evolution that humans need to be aware of the 'ferocity' of the deity and need to keep their distance unless they, too have unwavering dedication to their own spiritual evolution. Otherwise, if the human is still dually focused on their earthly life, the deity may cause the individual unwanted challenges, perhaps even death. Not because they seek to harm humans, but because they are so entranced in their spiritual fury to cleanse negativity that they might accidentally seek to cleanse an aspect of the human personality to which the human being is still firmly attached. The unexpected removal of such a thing may cause premature death to the person who may not be ready for such intense spiritual liberation.

Woden was also the god of spiritual initiation and deep wisdom. As such, Woden was considered the head of the pantheon. Woden eventually took the place of the Sky Father among the Germanic tribes. By the time of the Roman conquest, the Germanic tribes had replaced Tiw as the Sky Father with Woden as the "all-father." This shift in focus shows that by the time of the Roman occupation of Europe, spiritual awareness had become the primary focus of pre-Christian Germanic animism.

The concept of the "shaman" who accesses the spiritual dimensions through psychic traveling was very deeply ingrained into European consciousness. It is for this reason that I believe Western animist seekers are drawn to practices such as Siberian Tengerism which focus so heavily on astral travel or "shamanic journeying."

In any case, Westerners need not look far at all to find the European equivalent of the "shaman." Woden has been teaching ecstatic spiritual consciousness to Europeans for thousands of years. Woden, of course is only one example. If you are drawn to other European cultures, there are ample examples of practices involving spiritual ecstacy or "shamanism." All one needs to do is a little research to find them.

Medicine Wheels
Easily one of the most popular, cool and controversial focuses of neo-shamanism is Medicine Wheel practices. Medicine Wheels are also called "sacred hoops."

Sacred hoops vary from tradition to tradition, but what they all share in common is their use as a spiritual and energetic compass. The cardinal directions are used to balance oneself on multiple levels. Each direction has it's own totem, energy, color, etc...

It is not my intention to attempt to explain all the intricacies of Medicine Wheel teachings. For one reason, there are varying teachings out there. It seems each tradition has a different take on what each direction means and there are different color placements for different teachers. This, of course, doesn't take into account the many appropriated

Medicine Wheel teachings claiming to be of Native American origin that are not authentic.

But, the concept of the sacred wheel is definitely not unique to Native Americans, hence there is no need to appropriate their symbols to deeply enjoy the teachings connected to sacred circles.

Examples of European Sacred Circles include:
Stonehenge
Stone Circles
The Celtic Cross
Odin's Cross
The Aegishjalmur
The Elf Cross
Sun Wheel
The list goes on and on...

In Indo-European terms, the sacred circle is a very in-depth science. The Vedic and Hindu sciences of Yantra and Mandala are very intricate. There are literally thousands of different yantras and mandalas for specific spiritual purposes.

 Perhaps the most well known example of European sacred circles would be Stonehenge in England. Stonehenge and the surrounding area has been used as a sacred site for at least 10,000 years. It started out

as a circle of tree trunks aligned to different solar and lunar events such as solstices and equinoxes. As I mentioned earlier, Stonehenge has been recently determined to have been associated with ancestor worship. Stone Circles can be found all over Europe in both Celtic and Germanic countries.

 The Celtic cross, Odin's cross and the Elf Cross all have virtually identical shapes and purposes. When constructed with stones, they appear identical to the stereotypical Native American Medicine Wheel.

 The Aegishjalmur (Helmet of Awe) is one of the most powerful sacred wheel symbols in pre-Christian Europe. Viking warriors would paint this symbol on the 3rd eye region of their forehead in order to gain invincibility in battle. This is a very old IE symbol is also found in Vedic India where it is called an "ashtanga yantra" which means "eight limbed vehicle." In both the Indian and Germanic instances, this symbol was used as a very powerful tool for spiritual cleansing and protection. It was used extensively by Germanic tribes in Europe as far away as Iceland. This symbol, in my opinion must be at least 25,000 years old, perhaps much, much older.

Sun Wheel
The picture to the left is an eight spoked sun-wheel I constructed for ritual purposes in my front yard. To the average eye, this might appear as a "medicine wheel." But, our IE ancestors have been using these sun wheels for thousands of years. Sacred Hoops are an integral part of European animism. Instead of appropriating Native American symbols and names, we can employ this powerful spiritual tool from within our own heritage and achieve the same results.

Vision Quest
In neo-shamanism, the vision quest idea is borrowed from the practice of some Native American tribes involving spiritual initiation. In the vision quest, the individual isolates himself in Nature until he receives a vision that shows him his spiritual purpose in life. Such initiatory rites may include ingesting hallucinogenic plants, starvation or other kinds of physical stress which help to make one more susceptible to altered states of consciousness in order to receive a spiritual vision.

This practice was widely used in pre-Christian Europe. One such example from my ancestral tradition was called "sitting out." The individual would go out into the wilderness until they made contact with a spirit who would answer questions. Often times, sitting out was done in order to contact ancestor spirits for spiritual information.

Myths Concerning White People and Shamanism

OK, so I think I've done a pretty good job of confronting racial stereotypes by white people against Native Americans. But, what about the reverse? In the campaign to protect Native American spirituality, has there arisen any false racial stereotypes concerning European descended people in connection to "shamanism?"

The answer is "Yes." Let me address a few persistent myths concerning white people and shamanism.

Sweat Lodges

According to some, only Native Americans are allowed to practice sweat lodges for spiritual purposes. While I would agree that such sweat ceremonies containing Native American symbols, stories or rituals without permission should not be encouraged, it is unreasonable to assume that sweating practices were never practiced by Europeans.

Our modern "steam baths" were not appropriated from Native Americans. There is a very long record of using steam baths in Europe. It is very reasonable to assume that at one point in time, these practices had a spiritual significance. As with all animist practices in Europe, any spiritual connection would have been erased during conversion to Christianity.

I have experienced the benefits of sweat lodges myself. I have had some powerful spiritual experiences every time I have 'sweated.' To be clear, I have never attended a sweat that was facilitated by a Native American. Each time the facilitator was white. The sweat worked anyway. The Universe did not deny any of us the spiritual blessing because of our race. As with every other animist practice I have investigated, those benefits were never denied to me because of my racial heritage. I believe that anyone who wishes to benefit from this practice should have the right to do so. All that is needed is to avoid re-creating "Native American" style sweat lodges. Perhaps a ritual to European deities for guidance before a sweat would also help for obvious reasons.

I would also agree with Native Americans that sweat ceremonies should not be conducted for profit. To my knowledge, the majority of times that people have been injured in sweat ceremonies has been when someone was seeking to aggrandize themselves while seeking a financial profit. The fact that such people who were abusing this sacred practice were of European descent is not the point. In my experience with sweat lodges, anyone healthy enough and employing common sense while keeping themselves hydrated can enjoy this practice safely.

Shamanic Drumming

I have heard more than once that white people who practice trance drumming or "shamanic drumming" are appropriating this practice from native cultures.

Trance drumming can be found in every culture on the planet. The stereotype that Europeans never engaged in trance drumming is just plain false. A clay drum was found in Moravia (central Europe) that dates back to 6,000 B.C. In Anglo-Saxon England, during the Christian conversion period, English church authorities sent out instructions for local Christian priests to discourage parishioners from listening to traveling drum ensembles whose drum rhythms were believed to summon demons. The traveling drum ensemble reflects a pre-Christian tradition where drums were important in Anglo-Saxon pagan worship. Medieval music has a type of hand drum instrument that is almost identical in shape and construction to Cuban bongos. If you get a chance to listen to a traditional medieval musical troupe, you may get to see and hear this drum being played.

The Frame Drum

The drum most associated with neo-shamanism is the frame drum. Frame drums for trance drumming are usually associated with Siberian Tengerism and

Native American spirituality. However, frame drums have been and still are used extensively in Europe. One example is the Irish Bodhran. Most cultures in the world have some form of frame drum.

The Sami tribes in Scandinavia were using frame drums for "shamanic journeying" up until the 1700's. *(picture on left shows a Sami "noaide" animist priest with a large frame drum, circa early 1700s).*

Battle Drums
European armies were using drummers in battle before the "discovery" of the New World. The fact that unarmed drummers would march in front of advancing troupes on the battlefield shows how revered drummers were in Europe. The idea that drums would be used in battle also reveals the lingering pre-Christian animist belief that drums had the ability to disempower the enemy while strengthening ones own troops. While it is reasonable to assume that by the 1700's the battle-field drummer was considered purely symbolic, it nevertheless lends evidence to the idea that drums have had a long history with Europeans as a "shamanic" weapon.

Native American Flutes

The Native American flute (NAF) is very popular all over the world and are extremely popular among neo-shamans. The NAF is a "fipple" style flute that is tuned to the pentatonic minor scale. The European recorder and the penny whistle are also examples of fipple style flutes but use the standard major scale. "Fipple" just means that it is a whistle-style flute that anyone can play with very little experience as opposed to the end-blown or side blown flutes which take considerable practice to learn. To be accurate, there are also Native American flutes in existence that are not fipple flutes, but they are much less known. The iconic sound of the fipple style NAF has been associated with tribal animism and is a favorite instrument among neo-shamans. I myself love playing the NAF for ritual purposes.

While the actual design of NAFs are unique to indigenous North Americans, the iconic pentatonic minor scale played on them is not. As it turns out, the pentatonic minor scale was standardized onto NAFs in the late 20th century by Michael Graham Allen who was instrumental in bringing NAFs into their current popularity. Before the standardization of the minor pentatonic scale, Native American flute scales varied greatly. There was no standard NAF scale. They were often played very differently in times past.

The oldest recordings of NAFs by Native flute masters sounded *nothing* like modern NAF music. The scale was completely different. The flutes in those recordings had metal slivers in the sound chamber that made them sound more like trumpets than flutes. The tunes played on them were very fast and furious. A far cry from the slow, meditative modern NAF music that we commonly hear today.

It is more accurate to call the standardized, modern NAFs and music to be a Native and European-American hybrid.

I play modern NAF flutes myself. When teaching people how to play them, I point out that they are much easier to learn than side-blown flutes. In teaching, I will point out that these flutes are basically constructed like whistles. This is simply a fact. That is what all "fipple" flutes are. This is also true of the European recorder and the penny whistle. A fipple flute is one that you simply blow into the end to get the sound. It requires very little technique. It is the same technique used when you blow a whistle.

However, I have been sharply criticized more than once by Native Americans when I compare NAFs to whistles. I have gotten emails from angry Natives who viewed some of my youtube instructional videos on NAF playing who say, *"It is not a 'whistle!' It is sacred medicine. How dare you denigrate our sacred traditions by calling our flutes a whistle!"* Throw in a few racial insults against "white" people and you have the basic gist of these angry emails. There is no shame in the word 'whistle.' It is just an accurate description of the construction and explains why it is easier to play than other flutes.

The inference in those angry emails is that Native American flutes are purely sacred, spiritual instruments and European musical instruments are not. (i.e., it's OK for me to call a penny whistle a "whistle" but not an NAF). European fipple style flutes like recorders have been used for ceremonial purposes in churches dating back to the middle ages. How are they any less sacred than NAFs?

Perhaps since the construction of the NAF is unique to Native Americans that this is yet another symbol of Native American culture that Natives understandably want to preserve as their own.

But, I do wish to address the myth that this type of "shamanic" flute is unique to Native Americans. Flutes of all styles have been used by all cultures in the world.

The oldest flutes in the world were found in Germany. They are 35,000 years old. Some of these Paleolithic European flutes were tuned to a pentatonic scale. So, when we play modern NAFs, the scale we are using is the same scale that was used by our Paleolithic European ancestors.

Yet, there is still some controversy surrounding whites playing NAFs and as I have discovered, some Natives can be easily offended in regard to whites making or playing them.

Nevertheless, the NAF is a good place to start for the newbie who wants to integrate flute playing into their animist rituals simply because of their ease of playing and their beautiful, meditative tone. Once someone has learned the basics of the NAF and they wish to learn some more challenging flutes, there are more options available.

I used to play NAFs a lot more than I do now. One reason is that every time I pick up my NAFs to play them, I am reminded of some of the cruel racist comments I have received by some Natives who seem to think that these flutes are somehow cheapened simply because a "white" man touched them. I understand that this is just racism and I shouldn't pay attention to it. But, racism is just so ugly to me and I really do wish to be respectful. I cannot in good conscience do something that may be disrespectful to someone else's tradition. Besides, I just don't want to put all the effort into the mental gymnastics necessary in trying to forget what some have said. The positive side is that those hurtful comments motivated me to find some really, really cool alternative flutes that are connected to my own ancestry.

Other Flute Options for Ritual
If someone wanted to avoid any controversy and still get the benefits of playing an easy to learn flute for ritual purposes, they could simply play the penny whistle. If one wanted to stay true to their European Paleolithic ancestors, there are reconstructed flutes available that have a beautiful pentatonic scale. These are end-blown flutes, however that are much more difficult to learn than fipple styles.

Another option for authentic European flutes that are both very old and easy to play is the "willow flute" AKA the "overtone flute." This style of flute is said to be 100,000 years old and may be the first musical instrument played by humans. Most cultures have some form of overtone flute. Europe is no exception. Willow flutes have been played in Europe for thousands of years. In Scandinavia, it is believed that the overtone flute is played by trolls in the forest who use their music to hypnotize and lure unsuspecting humans into their realm.

Penny whistles can easily be found at local music stores or online. There are a number of really cool authentic European flute styles available on the internet if someone does any searching.

Here are some traditional European flute resources:
http://www.eriktheflutemaker.com
Look for the "Ice Age Flute" and the "Stone Age Flute"

http://www.naturinstrumenter.no
Some very cool traditional Scandinavian flutes

http://www.soundwell.com/stick-e.htm
An inexpensive European overtone flute

A Time For Healing
Native Americans have accused white culture of
abandoning the Earth - that we no longer
understand how to live in balance with Nature. I and
many, many white people completely agree (at least
in regard to some white people). Is there a way that
Natives can protect their culture and still share their
wisdom with those who clearly and desperately
want what they have?

I have tried to make the case in this book that I
wholeheartedly agree with the Native American
perspective on the issue of spiritual and cultural
appropriation. I can understand how the very
painful recent history of oppression, brutality and
genocide by Europeans on Natives would result in
a fierce desire by Natives to protect any and all of
their traditional cultures and religions.

I completely agree with many Natives who are
quick to point out how whites do not respect Nature.
I am the first to acknowledge that the core of the
'white' psyche has been deeply damaged and that
our modern culture as a whole has become
soulless. Natives seem to grasp that this emptiness

within white culture is what drives white people to appropriate Native spirituality.

So here's what I don't understand: It would make sense to me for Natives to be secretive about their spirituality if, like in times past, the U.S. gov't was seeking to swoop in and destroy their religion. But that is not the case any longer. Now you have white people begging to follow Native American spiritual paths. These white people would do anything they possibly could to preserve Native traditions. I'm not saying that Natives need whites to preserve their culture. But I am saying that whites are no longer seeking to destroy Native spirituality. They want to practice it. As rude and presumptuous as that may be, there is a difference between wanting to destroy something outright and naively wanting to practice something and inadvertently stepping all over it.

If Natives can see that whites are spiritually empty and hurting, why not help? If you can see that the destruction of Mother Earth is happening because of the gnawing spiritual chasm within peoples' souls, and now these very same people are seeking to gain the knowledge that you claim to own that protects the Earth, why are you refusing to share your wisdom with them? If for no other reason than to educate whites on how to respect the Earth, why not teach those who seek you out?

I have heard the argument from Natives that they aren't hiding their knowledge, they just don't like their culture and ceremonies being appropriated *without permission*. They say they would be happy to share their knowledge if only they were asked politely. Yet, how does one ask? What about the average white person who gets all their information from books and internet and does not live near or know any Natives? How are they supposed to find you to ask if you don't make yourselves available? Is it reasonable to expect these people to drive on to Native reservations and walk around asking for the local spiritual elder? (I realize this probably does happen, so I'm not advocating this approach.)

Listen, I looked for authentic Native teachings for years and couldn't find any. I found a few sincere and seemingly knowledgeable white people who claimed to have been taught by Natives and then of course there are all those "Native American Shamanism" books and the charlatans out there. I finally gave up many years ago. If given the opportunity, I would have asked politely. There was no one to ask...

I must be honest and say that I find it somewhat hypocritical of Natives to criticize whites for spiritual ignorance, but when these same whites seek to be taught wisdom from those same Natives, they are denied, seemingly, just because of their race. And then when these same whites out of desperation try to create their own version of Native teachings gleaned from whatever sources they can find, they are sharply criticized and accused of theft. Of course, charlatans are going to come in and fill the void. There is huge demand and you guys are not sharing! Somebody's gotta do it.

As someone who is also a keeper of sacred wisdom, I am very aware how dangerous powerful traditional ceremonies and practices can be if done improperly or without the necessary respect. It can be lethal. But there are ways to teach introductory rituals and teachings that can be done safely. As wisdom keepers, it is our responsibility to make spiritual teachings available to those who honestly and respectfully seek them.

It seems to me that the reason for our current dynamic is that Natives may still be hurting and angry over the very real brutality and theft that has been visited upon them by whites in recent history.

Nevertheless, the Earth is in serious peril. The danger we face concerning the state of our ecosystem is more important than any hurt feelings. I am not trying to minimize the pain. I know there are Natives still alive today who who have lived through some very nasty abuse. I don't pretend to understand that.

But, I am saying that it is time for all of us to grow up and move past it. If you want apologies, many whites will gladly apologize and have already done so. If Natives are the spiritually mature ones as many claim, then you have a responsibility to the less spiritually advanced to make your knowledge available to help them. Especially if, as many claim, that Native wisdom is necessary for the well-being of the planet. Let's all grow up and start the real healing. The Earth needs it.

Listen, spiritual appropriation of Native spirituality isn't going to stop. It is just too attractive to those who are unconsciously yearning for their own animist roots. Better to accept this unavoidable fact and do something to help, then to sit at home and complain about it or heap racial insults at them for seeking spiritual fulfillment. I and a few others are trying our best to provide an authentic alternative for whites. You are welcome to join us. If we can stand together as wisdom keepers and show people that our commonalities outnumber our differences, we can go a lot further in healing the Earth.

Having said that, Native Americans are not responsible for the fact that Europeans abandoned their own ancestral traditions. But, it should be a warning to other cultures who are in danger of losing their spiritual traditions. Many Native tribes have already adopted monotheist religion and many tribes no longer practice their ancestral spirituality or even speak their ancestral language. What happened to my ancestors can happen to you also. This disease is no respecter of race.

Even though I believe that some Native Americans are being somewhat immature and hypocritical in their criticism of whites who wish to learn from them, perhaps it ends up serving us both best if whites focus on their own animist heritage. Perhaps this is the reason that the Universe has not urged Natives to take a more active role in sharing their Earth Wisdom openly. It is not constructive for us to become dependent on others for our own spiritual healing.

I am aware that much of what I have said here may be offensive to both whites and Natives alike. If we are to heal, we need to be honest. The animist understanding is that Life is a two-way street. The only way for true healing and reconciliation is through honest talk.

Any authentic Native wisdom keepers reading this that understand what I am saying and the spirit with which I am saying it and want to help me spread the message, you are welcome to contact me. I am not interested in teaching Native practices, my goal is to create an alliance with fellow wisdom keepers of all traditions and work together to educate people on our shared animist heritage. I would love to see ancestral teachers from all cultures encourage everyone to preserve ancestral wisdom.

Reintegrating Our Pre-Christian Animism
All of the historical information out there about our pre-Christian ancestors and their beliefs and

practices is all well and good, but how does one learn how to do these things?

Authentic animism is not just a set of intellectual beliefs like most modern religions, it is a set of skills, skills that must be taught just like any other art like music, martial arts, etc... Most people cannot simply choose to immediately know the particulars of how to practice these things.

Every learned subject has to have a context from within which someone learns the specifics. As a martial artist, I am aware that the only way to become effective at self-defense is by learning directly from someone with experience. No skilled martial artist ever learned his craft from books or videos. True skill in this area is only accomplished from learning one-on-one with a skilled practitioner. The same is true for animist spiritual practices.

One of the main problems I have observed with much of the new-age practices is that, often times it smacks to me of mere intellectualized fantasy. Since we Westerners no longer have much experience with these animist spiritual arts, we understandably feel insecure. We still carry a strong belief instilled into us by this separatist "scientific" culture that we live in which teaches us that all this stuff is merely something that lives in our fantasies. We treat animist spiritual practices as something that we use merely as subjective, psychological self-help. So, as a result, our attempts at animism tend to be restricted to our fantasy lives.

As someone who has trained and practiced animist arts from within lineages that retain an unbroken connection into prehistory, I can tell you there is a HUGE difference in practical effectiveness between some of our new-age practices and authentic practices with an unbroken history.

We Westerners have lost touch with our ancient traditions, so it is only natural that those who are serious about finding practices with real-world effectiveness seek out cultures that still practice these arts and can teach us the practical know-how necessary to achieve success.

So, I do understand the need to find qualified instruction. I am well aware that many of the available courses and seminars in "shamanism" have a very real effectiveness. One example is Michael Harner's courses in "core-shamanism." although many accuse him of spiritual appropriation, I have no doubt that he has learned from authentic sources. I also have no doubt that many students of core-shamanism have very real, effective skills.

I traveled a similar route as many "core shamans." Although I did not train in Siberian "shamanism," the power and effectiveness of my current practices is derived from my initial training in Taoist, Vedic and African animist practices. After training in those fields and subsequently contacting my own ancestral spiritual teachers, I have been able to transfer the power and practical experience from those foreign animist practices and apply them to better understand the beliefs and practices of my animist ancestors.

So, I do not begrudge anyone from training in authentic, foreign animist practices. But, my hope is that we can use that practical knowledge gleaned from those foreign practices and use them to help us reawaken the beautiful, rich animist heritage within our own pre-Christian European culture.

This may sound as though I am proposing some kind of animist ethnic exclusivity. I am not. My reasoning is practical. In my experience, when I was learning foreign animist practices, I had to put a huge amount of time and effort into learning foreign languages, symbology , etc. While I did end up learning very effective spiritual practices, the nature of the arts I learned always had a "foreign" feeling to them and I always felt like a spiritual outsider, a spiritual "tourist" if you will. I put a lot of time and energy into translating many concepts into my own language and cultural frame of reference in order to make it more relevant to me. As a result, I was always aware of my ethnic difference. I often felt embarrassed of my own ancestry. I always felt a separation that seemed to hinder my progress.

After spiritual and academic research into the animism of my ancestors, I began integrating my experience in my varied animist traditions into my own ancestral practices. When I did so, my effectiveness as an animist priest skyrocketed. One reason was that I no longer had to reinterpret animist concepts into my own language or cultural frame of reference. I already had the cultural knowledge of Elves, Dwarves, Wizards, Witches, Magick, etc., in my cultural mythology.

Once I understood that animism was not something that only foreigners practiced, I was able to live my animism more fully in every moment. The other added benefit was that I was able to consciously access the spiritual power of my ancestors in a more immediate and palpable way than ever before.

Before integrating my ancestral animist identity, there was always a schism within me between my foreign spirituality and my "white" cultural identity. That has now vanished. It has been a real 'soul retrieval' experience.

However, some of you may be feeling that I am just being a "buzz-kill." You may be very attached to your Native American style Shamanism.

"So, what's the harm?" You may ask. *"Why can't I just enjoy my spirituality? So, what if I choose to worship Spirit in the style of Native Americans or*

Siberians? It's all the same anyway. Right? Why can't you all just leave me alone and let me worship in my own way?"

That is a very good question. I certainly do not begrudge anyone any practice especially if they have permission from a recognized spiritual teacher.

But, if you are a self-styled shaman, I am willing to bet that you believe that the main problem with modern society is the destruction of the planet. Right? Then, if you also, like me, want to change the destructive thought patterns in modern society that are responsible for global warming, the rampant destruction of Nature, the loss of wild places, etc... Then it is vitally important that we reintegrate these concepts back into our own culture.

By respecting the wishes of Native Americans and Siberians to stop using their symbols as a context for our desire to practice animism, we allow these concepts to be found from within our own cultural framework. This will more easily help the shift in consciousness necessary. Otherwise, we simply look like "liberal, hippy, new age, tree-huggers." We look like aberrations rather than what we really are which is the true conservatives seeking to reintegrate traditional European values of: Respecting Nature and Honoring our Ancestors.

As long as "white" people continue to appropriate the practices of other cultures without permission, they not only demean and dilute those cultural practices but, they perpetuate a very destructive racial stereotype that exacerbates racial and spiritual bigotry.

But there is an even more important practical reason to stop spiritual appropriation. Because failing to do so will actually create more destruction to the environment. Here's why...

As long as "white" people believe that "shamanism" is some foreign, exotic set of beliefs and practices that only belong to other cultures, then Western society will always view these beliefs to be an exotic, foreign oddity that we use for entertainment purposes. People will always see Earth Wisdom as something "different." It will be viewed as an interesting, cute, foreign mindset that they can turn on and off at their convenience. They can go to a weekend seminar, play "shaman" and release some tension and then come home, put back on their modern, "white person" persona and revert back to the "normal" Western way of life. Isn't this what many people are already doing?

Those of us who are deeply dedicated to returning the human race back to the Natural, Healing ways of Earth, will always be viewed as strange and different unless this ancestral, animist path can be wholly identified with the culture in which we now live.

Does that make sense? Part of our job as Earth Wisdom keepers is to remind modern Western society of its true origins. If modern, Western, "white" folks come to understand that their natural, ancestral traditional way of life is one of animism, then people will seek it out and more readily integrate animism back into our society. We will be able to integrate Earth Wisdom back into our subconscious minds and live this philosophy every minute of every day as opposed to just once a year on "earth day."

If people think animism is only from "primitive" cultures, then they will not know that they use these traditional European animist concepts every day in their language. They will not know the power of "Weird" even though they use that word every day. They will not know that the "Lord of The Rings" trilogy is not just a cute fairy tale. Tolkien's intention for his work was to be a powerful animist European mythology for modern times. He spent years constructing his mythological world through painstakingly researching ancestral, pre-Christian Germanic animism. The reason his work is so popular is because it is derived our ancestral mythology. People respond to it because the beliefs in those books and films are embedded in our ancestral memories and even in our DNA.

If you have become a shaman because you want to be a warrior for the Earth and reverse the damage we have done to Her, then you owe it to yourself, your family, your country and your ancestors to embrace the teachings they upheld for 50,000 years.

Our materialist, racist, separatist, modern culture is NOT our traditional way of life. It was imposed upon our animist ancestors by greedy, imperial politicians who appropriated an incomplete understanding of Gnostic Christian philosophy to further their political control.

They warped Gnostic spiritual philosophy and used it as a justification to eradicate animism from the European mindset in order to better control people and gain more wealth and power.

(OK... I'm getting off of my soapbox. At least for the moment.)

Of course, you are free to choose whatever cultural practice that speaks to you. If you choose not to embrace ancestral European practices, then at least be sure that you have permission for whatever practice you adopt in order to help bring legitimacy back to animism.

Where To Go From Here

If you are in need of direction for Earth-friendly practices that are openly available, here are a few resources that I recommend.

The Thunder Wizard Path
www.ThunderWizard.com
The Thunder Wizard Path is a solitary path I have created designed to reconstruct a modern form of authentic Teutonic animist mysticism. The pre-Christian Germanic equivalent of "shaman" is the word "wizard" which simply means "Wise One." While there are other neo-Germanic polytheist religious organizations in existence, this path is more focused on animism and mysticism rather than organized religion. The website contains a lot of information, rituals and Life Force exercises in a traditional Teutonic animist context.

Sun Wheel Magick
www.Sun-Wheel-Magick.com
Sun-Wheel-Magick is my attempt at a more general approach to animism and mysticism with a decidedly Indo-European approach. But I also introduce the animist similarities shared by multiple authentic animist traditions from around the world. The website contains a free introductory course in using the sun-wheel (IE version of the "medicine wheel") as an introduction into hands-on animism using the eight directions of the Sun-Wheel.

Druidry

http://www.druidry.org

The Order of Bards, Ovates and Druids is probably
the most well-known of the modern Druidry groups.
Those interested in an authentic, modern Celtic
form of animism will enjoy this group (especially
those who are drawn to Native American style
animism). They have extensive courses, books and
other material for those who prefer an open, Celtic-
derived animist path.

The Troth

www.TheTroth.org

The Troth is an Asatru organization that promotes
modern neo-heathenism. (Asa-tru means "True to
the gods.") Asatru is a form of neo-heathenism that
emerged during the 1960s and 1970s. While the
Troth as an umbrella organization is more focused
on reconstruction of pre-Christian Germanic
polytheist religion, there are also many folks in the
Troth who practice various forms of Germanic
animism and mysticism and as a rule, I find the
majority of Troth-ers to be very open minded and
friendly.

There are, of course, many more paths available to
you, but these are a good start for those seeking
authentic, Western, pre-Christian animist paths. If
you do a bit of searching, you will surely find many
more options available to you.

Whatever your eventual spiritual destination, I wish you well and may the ancestors of us all guide and bless you.

Peace.

About The Author

Michael William Denney has been researching, practicing and teaching animist (shamanic) disciplines from around the globe for over 20 years. He has authored two books: "The Thunder Wizard Path" and "Wealth Shaman" as well as a third book, "Mounting Sleipnir -Reviving European Polytheist Animism" which will be released soon. He has also released numerous instructional DVDs in meditation and animism as well as numerous CDs in World Music.

Mr. Denney currently teaches Teutonic (Germanic) animism, Taoist internal martial arts and mysticism, qigong, Vedic mantra and mysticism, meditation and West African animist drumming. For more info go to: www.ThunderWizard.com

28821720R00052

Made in the USA
Lexington, KY
04 January 2014